THE
CRYSTAL
BOOK

Cover design   Kathi Van de Kieft
Editing and layout   Carol Hewitt
Illustrations   John Cassone

First Printing August 1983

Second Printing October 1983

Third Printing November 1983

Fourth Printing March 1984

Fifth Printing August 1984

Sixth Printing April 1985

Seventh Printing August 1985

Eighth Printing October 1985

Ninth Printing March 1986

Tenth Printing September 1986

Eleventh Printing May 1987

Twelfth Printing July 1987

Thirteenth Printing October 1987

Fourteenth Printing April 1988

Published by The Crystal Company,
P.O. Box 348, Sunol, CA 94586

Library of Congress
Number 84-70659

ISBN Number
0-9614094-0-1

I dedicate this book
to the master,
Frank R. (Nick) Nocerino,
the biggest crystal of them all.

Contents

Introduction

"I received my first quartz crystal at about the age of five or six. I read and studied nearly all of the works on stones that I could find. George Frederick Kunz and William T. Fernie M.D. were my favorites."

Crystal Gazing
Theodore Besterman

The last book that seemed to have any pertinent information on crystal awareness was Theodore Besterman's "Crystal Gazing." His book was concise and dealt with who used crystals and why. This book apparently took Besterman to many countries to see how crystals were used. But as complete as his work was, Mr. Besterman never took the reader through the how of using a crystal. A lot of research has, over the years, gone into who and why but these researchers seemed to be caught up in crystal gazing (or scrying) and never went any further into the many other uses of crystals. Crystal interest seems to run in flurries, and the last 10 years have shown a large group of serious researchers, investigators, teachers, and practitioners of crystal awareness. These interested parties have gone far beyond the gazing stage.

As a person who has worked with crystals since I was a child and started to teach crystal awareness in 1948, I have never met a more serious student or researcher than Dale Walker. I admire and respect his work.

I remember when he first came to my classes, bringing a sincerity that has grown continuously over the years.

Dale listens and does the things that you teach him, then goes further and experiments with his own investigations and research.

This has opened up many levels of consciousness, bringing in vast amounts of new knowledge that Dale put to the test of experiment and investigation. Soon much information was coming in that had to be verified. Dale was looking for more serious researchers and investigators. He found the answer, as I had 40 years ago, in teaching. He compiled what he was learning and taught it to others, involving them in the research and experiments.

This book summarizes over five years of such research by Dale and his many students all over the United States and Canada, and includes many of the conclusions that my work has shown.

Most important of all, this book is for everyone who has ever wanted to learn about their own energies and the extension of that energy by the use of natural quartz crystal; mainly because this book tells the how of crystal awareness. All of the exercises have been tested over and over and then broken down into simple workable terms for the serious student to use.

I believe it took courage for Dale Walker to put this work together in a time of material importance. Those who take this work seriously will find extensions of themselves beyond the norm. As faith makes men into giants, so must faith in each of you be used in your work to learn and use the crystal. As holy books are tools that cause man to extend himself, so too is the crystal. The only difference being that here you can see, feel, taste, smell, and hear the difference. If you are the type of student who fully desires to extend his or her God-given gifts, this book will open many of the doors and take you along many beautiful roads of your inner self. The question is: do you have that courage, or desire to grow beyond the material realm? If you do, let us know how, and where, you go. Feel free to exchange your thoughts with us or others, so that we may all grow together. The crystal is being rediscovered. Let's rediscover it together.

F. R. "Nick" Nocerino

It is with deep gratitude that I speak for this student and layman's introduction to crystals.

When one has known scores of healers, from the world-famous to the backyard neighbors, it is truly refreshing to work with Dale Walker.

We who have studied with him in classes and individually have found him unpretentious, completely honest and conscientious. The airy comments and suggestions he offers are all based on solid, proven experience. His sense of humor keeps everyone around from becoming stodgy and self-important. But he never allows his students to lose sight of the fact that our Creator made miracles and wonders possible through crystals.

You can depend on this work, for it is clear, valid and practical.

October, 1982   Gladys R. Graham
Lafayette, Colo.   D.D., D.M.

Acknowledgements

It would be impossible to acknowledge all of the people who have encouraged me to write this book. Special thanks go to Nick Nocerino, Laurie Jelgersma, Ellie Blank, Janet Werfelmann, Gladys Graham, Sandra Bowen, Frances Herriman, Bruce and Marvyline Fraser, Eleanor Alford, my lovely daughter Kelly and her husband Doug Sandlin, my son Douglas Walker and his wife, Terry, for helping me see more clearly, and Derek Walker, the smallest crystal. Thanks to my fabulous new Crystal Awareness teachers, and all the crystal graduates, my new Light Family. A very special thanks to the crystal channeling group: Shirley, Eddie, Spiro, Jan and Bill. Most of all I thank Lord Michael and my spiritual guidance for staying with me, and the Crystal Brotherhood for choosing me to be their messenger. I continue to invoke the Christ within me that I may be a clear and perfect channel. Light be my Guide.   Da El

It is a practice among some cultures, at a point in spiritual evolution, to choose a new name representing your spiritual desire. I have rearranged the spelling to create a new spiritual name, Da El. It means, "Child of God".

Da El

Preface

Welcome to the world of crystals. This book is an invitation to explore a world within which can be manifested without. If this sounds mystical, we will set aside the mysticism. Let us explore the physical boundaries of the crystal and extend it into the metaphysical. The difference is not that great. It only requires that we use a new approach for the mind to comprehend.

We will deal mainly with the quartz family of crystals. Other crystals may be mentioned, but when we use the term "crystal," we mean quartz.

We will explore our practical uses of crystals as tools for mind energy. What can you do with this tool? Of what benefit can it be in your everyday life? We will look at simple techniques for reducing pain or removing headaches. You will find ways to charge water, stimulate plants, get better gas mileage, lower electrical costs, meditate, increase your intuitive abilities, gain energy, live a more productive and giving life, and most of all — gain meditative peace.

We will explore consciousness, consider psychic phenomena, creativity, intuition and learn to communicate with all of these.

Our major theme is healing in all its dimensions. Whether it be mental, emotional, physical or spiritual, balance is central to all concerns. Our goal is simple: heal the planet by healing ourselves.

None of the techniques we list are meant to be substitutes for conventional medical practice. Anyone under treatment by a doctor should continue as long as he is receiving positive results. We offer crystals as an experimental alternative tool for natural healing. We offer medical practitioners a different view of the human body as a series of energy systems with crystals as a device for adjusting and balancing these systems. Give your doctor a copy of this book.

There are many visualization exercises here and you may choose to record them on an audio tape and play it for yourselves. You will find the exercises much easier if your logical mind is not engaged in reading.

This book is in no way a scientific treatise. Many other researchers are studying the effects of crystals on human consciousness, using traditional methods with varying results. We are participating with the hope of establishing an area of communication between technologically-oriented people and those functioning more in the intuitive. We do not claim to have The Truth. We only offer our truth as we have experienced it.

Many people are coming forth now calling themselves crystal teachers. To avoid being filled with incorrect or incomplete information, we suggest you ask these questions: What is the scope of their research? Can they do what they teach? Who were their teachers? Can they transfer their experiences to you, so you can do it too?

Our information comes from an interesting process called "Intuitive Channeling," which was later proven through our collective group experiences. Try it and see if it works. If it does, it will be your truth and knowledge. We seek knowledge, not data. Information can only be knowledge when it is experienced. Until then it is just information.

This book is designed to start you on your path. How far you go will depend on your own perseverance and discipline. May all your experiences be valuable enough to keep records and create the need to share them. We would like to hear from you.

Quartz Crystals

In my lectures and workshops, one question seems to be primary: What **are** crystals? The answer comes out many ways. Physically, crystals are fossilized water. They come into existence when water combines with an element in the presence of certain conditions of pressure, temperature and energy. When conditions are right, water will cause (or allow?) the element to grow as a crystal. (Metaphysically, water—the source of life—enables a member of the mineral kingdom to express itself as a more unified and ordered being, reaching for greater completion toward the universe.)

Silicon, as sand, combines with water to become silicon dioxide, or quartz crystal.

Crystals have certain physical properties; in the quartz crystal these properties are called piezoelectric, pronounced pie-ee-zo.

Quartz amplifies, transforms, stores, focuses, and transfers energy. A tiny slice of quartz in a microcircuit increases an electrical signal—this property gave birth to microphones, loudspeakers and all forms of audio and video equipment.

Quartz transforms energy. If squeezed, it generates electricity. When an electrical current is sent through it, it swells. An alternating current causes it to alternately swell and shrink. Done fast enough, this is called an oscillation. When cut in precise shapes, quartz vibrates at precise rates and transforms electricity into waves which can be broadcast as in radio and television signals.

Quartz changes solar energy into electricity in devices called photovoltaic cells.

It stores energy. A tiny slice of quartz in a microcircuit stores large amounts of data in the "memory" of a computer.

It is used to transmit information within computers and in intricate electronic switching functions. Its ability to vibrate at precise rates is used in the creation of extremely accurate timepieces.

QUARTZ CRYSTALS

Quartz focuses energy. In lasers, crystals allow us to measure the distance to the moon in seconds, burn through steel walls or perform delicate eye surgery.

METAPHYSICAL PROPERTIES

In metaphysics, all of the physical properties have counterparts in the mental or psychic world. Perhaps we should expand the definition of metaphysics. Meta means "above or beyond." Metaphysics, then, would be above and beyond physics. If physics is, eventually, the study of the action of energy, nothing can be above and beyond it, since everything is energy in some form. Can we then separate a part of it and call it "Mind Physics," the study of the action of the energies of the mind?

Crystal's effects on mental energy are as dramatic as its effects on physical energy.

Amplify. Not only do the crystals amplify body energy but thoughts as well. They create power and clarity in thinking. They enable thoughts to more effectively influence matter. Set aside two plants of equal size and type. Using the same methods of feeding and watering, put a crystal next to one plant. Put nothing by the other. With a crystal in your left hand picture in your mind the first plant growing tall and strong. Talk to the plant and describe how beautiful it is and will be. Fill it with warmth and affection. Do nothing with the other plant. Totally ignore it except to continue to feed and water it. The results will show a dramatic difference in the growth within one month.

Transform. Fill two cups of water from the faucet. Place one cup on a clear quartz crystal cluster about six inches in diameter. Place the other cup at least ten feet away. Leave for 24 hours. Taste the water in each cup. There should be a considerable difference in the taste of the water in each cup. The energy of the crystals will transform the molecular composition of the water.

Store. We can charge a crystal with energy and the crystal will store that energy for later use. Our experience has shown we can store information in a crystal. We do not have an adequate test to prove this. Remember in the Superman movie the crystal with all the knowledge which taught the baby and later the man? We are working on the techniques for recording and recovering thought-forms stored in crystals. As an example, consider the crystal skulls found in Central America and believed to be such storage computers by many crystal researchers. These researchers have seen visions of all ages and found that they have become aware of new knowledge after working with the crystal skulls.

Focus. With our thoughts we can focus energy precisely where we desire. With the crystal we can use this ability for healing. This is discussed in greater detail later.

Transfer. The crystal enables us to not only transfer energy directly to someone we are near, but to mentally broadcast anywhere at any distance to cause healing thousands of miles away. It is excellent for telepathy, the sending and receiving of thoughts.

Much more is possible. The crystal is a corridor between the physical dimension and the dimensions of the mind. We can use it to communicate with minerals, plants and animals. We can also communicate with intelligence outside the physical dimension. We can talk to angels, talk to masters, teachers, healers. Many of these have great wisdom to impart. They are eager to do so, but cannot until you have the means to listen. Some people have their inner hearing open and can and do receive. Others need help. The crystal can be the means to enable you to communicate.

It can create altered states of consciousness. A crystal can serve as a vehicle for reaching and operating talents and abilities of the mind. All of the psychic abilities can be stimulated and amplified by the use of the crystal. Its most effective metaphysical use is in healing. Here the crystal enables the metaphysical mind to direct the physical body to repair and balance itself. Thus, the crystal can be the vehicle through which the physical and metaphysical become united.

Atlantis

Thousands of books have been written about Atlantis. Only a few have mentioned crystals. Edgar Cayce, the trance medium of Virginia Beach, Virginia, mentioned them many times in his trance readings.

In her book Romance of Atlantis, Taylor Caldwell, at the age of 12, wrote of using crystals for rejuvenation, keeping people alive for hundreds of years.

Ruth Montgomery in The World Before spoke of the use of crystals in Atlantis and Lemuria.

Our research channeling spoke of a whole civilization of incredible power and splendor made possible by crystal science. Machines were merged with the power of the mind. Crystals were used to furnish unlimited free power. They were used to convert the sun's energy into a form of electricity. We saw pictures of alternating concave and convex lenses catching and changing the rays of the sun and storing the changed energy in a liquid material. We later identified this as a solution of liquid crystal.

Great grids were designed to capture and use the energy field of the earth. All were powered and made possible with crystals.

Through the use of controlled thought to direct the chemical changes of matter, huge crystals were grown in very exact shapes. Even the molecular design was changed to shape and direct energy in exact ways. Sound and light were mapped out in precise frequencies not only physical, but mental as well. These were fed through these designed crystals to power air, sea and undersea craft. The discovery of the use of crystals to control the incredible energy reaction between matter and anti-matter gave birth to space flight. When they linked this drive to the ability of the crystal to assist the mind to travel inter-dimensionally, they were able to design interstellar space craft and fly to the stars.

Crystals were used in construction. We saw a picture of a circle of people around a crystal. All of the people had been trained since childhood for perfect concentration. We could see a beam of energy travel miles away to a workman holding a box with a lever, a control stick on top. He pointed it at a huge stone, moved the lever and the stone rose and poised in the air. Another slight adjustment and he walked away, moving the stone in front of him.

Large towers like lighthouses were erected near the sea. Operators were stationed here to communicate with the dolphins, porpoises and whales. With their assistance the operators herded large schools of fish into waiting offshore nets.

Some of the priest-engineers talked to the deva spirits of the animal and vegetable kingdoms. With the deva's help they experimented to create new forms of life. Half vegetable, half animal, animals with wings or fish bodies were created. Some even merged animals and humans to create bird people, mermaids, minotaurs and centaurs. Nothing was impossible, for the crystal gave man dominion over the patterns of creation. They became like gods.

Mighty and beautiful healing temples filled the land. Here the combination of light, color, sound, magnetism and thought energies were channeled through crystals to create wonders in healing.

The Atlanteans mastered the intricacies of all the rays and sub-rays of color and sound. They mapped the neurological pathways of the human body and brain. They knew all the energy channels of the energy bodies. Etheric surgery on the energy body was preferable and more desirable than on the physical. When it was necessary, priest healers linked with the minds of the patients to direct the cells of the body to separate and expose an offending organ. Blood vessels were directed to close off. Cells around the organ released their hold and forced the organ to the surface of the body where the healer took it out and placed it in a rejuvenation chamber. When the organ was rebuilt it was replaced in the body. The cells reconnected themselves, the blood vessels sent blood back into the organ and the wound closed itself up. There was no pain, no bleeding, no infection and no shock.

Some perverted the great good the crystals were designed to do. The power of the crystals was used to destroy and enslave. The tremendous energies released caused an inbalance in the earth. A massive earthquake brought about the total destruction of Atlantis.

Some survivors took the crystals to other lands. In Egypt they built a towering pyramid, using crystals to lift and set the massive blocks.

They used the laser-like energy to cut and dress the blocks so precisely a folded piece of paper could not be passed between pieces of stone weighing tons. They made the base from granite, knowing the weight of the stones above would squeeze the quartz in the granite to generate an energy field which they used for healing, rejuvenation, and religious ceremonies. They sheathed it in sandstone and chalcedony to form a resonator and capped it with pure quartz. With this gigantic transmitter they were able to keep limited communication open with their friends in the Pleiades and the other star systems.

Wherever the survivors went they left records. They left them beneath the Great Pyramid in Egypt, in caverns in the Tibetan mountains, and in pyramids in China, South America and North America. Mountain peaks all over the world also have their depositories. They left tablets of a man-made stone, hard as diamond. They left books of gold and thousands of crystals.

The real information was in the crystals where 200,000 years of knowledge of one of the mightiest civilizations on earth was stored as 3-dimensional thought holograms. These crystals will be found and deciphered before the end of this century.

Cleansing & Other Basics

When you get a quartz crystal, some basics are suggested. First of all, a crystal should be cleansed. If it cannot be cleansed immediately, it should be cleared. Defining clearing and cleansing requires a certain amount of explanation.

The life field of a human is the strongest of all life fields, either organic or inorganic (organic being those containing carbon). After humans, in order of intensity, are the life fields of animals, vegetables and minerals.

When another person touches your crystal he leaves his own life field energy imprinted on the life field of the crystal. Everything which exists is an energy form. Within the imprint of the human life field is the emotional and mental energy level of that person at the time of imprint. Someone with a fine degree of sensitivity can touch the crystal and use the imprinted energy to tune in to the person who first touched it, and may receive impressions of the first person. This is called psychometry.

In a similar way, this emotional energy level can be received unconsciously by someone who is untrained in energy perception. He can take these emotions to be his own. If the first person touching the crystal is feeling sad, angry, hateful, or any inbalanced emotion, the second person can pick up these emotions and accept them as his own feelings. This can be extremely disturbing.

Another consideration is the possibility of an energy transfer. When you connect with the energy of someone else there is the chance that person can tap into and take your energy. Think of the simile of two batteries. If you connect two batteries of unequal charge, they will equalize. The highly charged one will come down and the lower charged one will come up. The same thing is true of people. You could be feeling full of energy and someone connected to you through your crystal could take that energy if he is lower than you.

To avoid this, the crystal should be cleansed to remove the imprinted energy. This can be done effectively by covering the crystal with sea salt for two to seven days. Sea salt can be found in most health food stores. If you prefer, you may submerge your crystal in a salt water solution of one half pound of sea salt to one gallon of water for the same period of time.

Less recommended methods would be to pass the crystal over the south pole of a large magnet to demagnetize it, or submerge it in a solution of four tablespoons of baking soda in a gallon of water. Another traditional cleansing solution is half brandy and half water. Next best is hot port or sherry brought to a boil, then shut off and allowed to sit. All of these should be used for a maximum of seven days.

As you can see, the simplest and most inexpensive method is salt. It has proven to be the most effective one we have tried. Experiment for yourself and pick the method you like the best.

Clearing & More Basics

If you cannot immediately cleanse your crystal, you can neutralize the energy by clearing it. Here is one way:

Close your eyes. Picture in your mind an energy meter, a half-round dial numbered from 0 to 100. Wherever you see the indicator needle, move it left to 0, neutralizing the old energy. Now move it all the way to the right to 100, and put your own energy into it. With your eyes still closed, look down at your waist and see a white ring of energy. This is your aura or energy field. Expand that ring out until it is at least a foot away. See it getting brighter and more clear until it is like a crystal ball all around you. Any negative emotion, like a dark arrow, when it strikes this shield will change to a white arrow of positive energy which you can use or send to others. Any time you hold your crystal and expand your aura it will automatically form a protective shield. Any negative or imbalanced energy, like a dark arrow, which strikes this shield will change to white, positive energy which you can use or send to others.   Continue to expand the light until the entire crystal is glowing with brilliant light. Now come out of the crystal and back into your body, back into this time and space. Open your eyes.

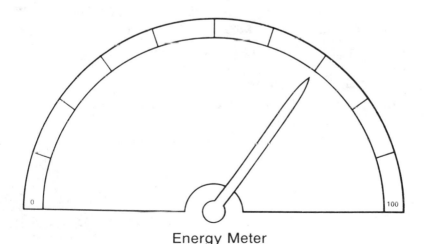

Energy Meter

When you become more at ease with your crystal you can also clear it with light.

Get yourself in a comfortable position with your crystal in your left hand. Close your eyes. See your crystal in front of you getting larger and larger until it is as big as a house. Go inside. Walk over and stand in the center of the room. From the center of your being see a light begin to glow. As it glows brighter and brighter, see it getting larger until the light surrounds your body. As it continues to expand it fills the room. All darkness moves out away from the light, for darkness cannot exist where the light is.

Use the clearing technique whenever you cannot easily cleanse it with salt. After you have cleansed it, you should not let any one touch your personal crystal. This is often a problem because of the attraction your crystal will have for others, especially your friends and family.

Here is a suggestion we have found to be effective. For the first seven days after you get your crystal, allow all your close acquaintances to admire and touch it. Within seven days you should see most of those who would feel close enough to you to touch it without your permission.

When the week is over, put your crystal in sea salt for seven days. After that, do not let anyone touch it. If someone does touch it by some circumstance, immediately clear it and put it in sea salt over night. The next day reactivate it again, using the clearing process and expanding the aura.

Treat your crystal as a dear and precious friend. Keep it in a small bag made of natural materials such as leather, cotton, silk, wool, linen and so on. If it is used for healing, wash it after each session. Periodically place it in salt overnight when it seems to be getting full. If it gets sticky or tacky, wash it with plain soap and water. Above all, know it is a living entity. Treat it with love and care and it will reward you with a lifetime of service.

Merging

To use your crystal most effectively, attune yourself to it. The closer your vibrations are to the crystal, the more effectively it will operate as a tool to enable you to control energy. Keep your crystal next to your body for 33 days. The constant interaction with your body will cause the crystal to synchronize its vibrations with yours. At the end of 33 days it will be totally yours.

Another method is to merge with it.

Get yourself in a comfortable position. Put your crystal in your left hand. Look at your crystal with the point up. See how it resembles a glass house with six sides and a peaked roof. Close your eyes and see your crystal with the point up. Come in closer and as you do, see the crystal getting larger until it is as large as a house. There is an open doorway. Feel yourself flow inside. Look around you. Light is coming through the ceiling, the apex of the crystal, and strikes the walls and floors. Do you see colors? What do the walls look like? How do the floors look? Do you see anything else inside? What is the temperature like? Is it warm, cold, hot, neutral? What do you feel? Listen carefully. What is that sound? What do you hear inside the crystal? Can you think of something which sounds like it? Take a deep breath. What do you smell? What does that odor remind you of? Remember all your impressions. Taste a piece of crystal. What is that taste? Can you compare it to anything you have tasted before? Run your hand against the side of the crystal, the wall. Is it smooth or rough? Soft or hard? Cool or warm? What sensations are you getting when you feel the surface of the wall?

With your hand still on the wall, begin to feel the crystal vibrating. As that vibration increases, feel your body vibrating with it until you feel yourself flowing into the crystal and you ARE the crystal. All of the energies which flow through the crystal are yours to command by your thoughts. You are the master of the crystal.

Every time you go into your crystal it will become easier and easier to do so. Every time you go into your crystal all your senses will be sharper and your impressions will be more precise. Stay in your crystal as long as you desire. When you want to come out, walk over to the doorway of the crystal. Step outside, back into your body, back into this time and space.

Enter the Crystal - Merging

Activating

A crystal can be activated in several ways. By activate, we mean to prepare the crystal to enable us to use it. The simplest method is to hold it in your left hand. In a short time the crystal will begin to pulse or vibrate in attunement with you. As soon as you feel this tingling or pulsing sensation, you can begin to use it. A more complete activation or attunement can be attained by using the merging technique of going into the crystal. Any mental activity used with the crystal will activate it. The clearing techniques and the aura expansion both qualify.

Always cleanse all crystals in salt before activating them. When you are sleeping during the 33-day merging period, tape the crystal to your left hand. Either keep it in your pocket or carry it around your neck in a pouch. At the end of the 33 days your vibrations will be in attunement with the crystal.

Charging

Pyramids can be used to charge crystals. Use a simple wire frame model of the great pyramid of Egypt. Orient your pyramid to magnetic North. Place the crystal in the center of the pyramid, one third of the distance up from the base to the apex. Orient the tip so it is pointing north. Keep it in the pyramid for 33 days.

Charged crystals can in turn be used to charge other crystals. Place them together for a maximum of 33 days. There will be a transfer of energy until both crystals are of equal strength.

Orgone accumulators made of alternating organic and inorganic materials can be used to charge crystals. Place the crystals in the accumulator for the required maximum of 33 days.

Crystals can be charged using magnets. Place the crystal on the south pole of the magnet. The higher the gauss field the greater the charge. A range of 1000 to 2000 gauss is good for an experiment. As you experiment with charging your crystals, you may note the tendency for your crystals to become more clear. The wispy cloudiness in the crystals is moisture. Constant exposure to an electromagnetic field seems to cause the moisture to disappear. The exact mechanics are not clear. Perhaps the field energy causes a molecular expansion, releasing the hydrogen and oxygen in the water.

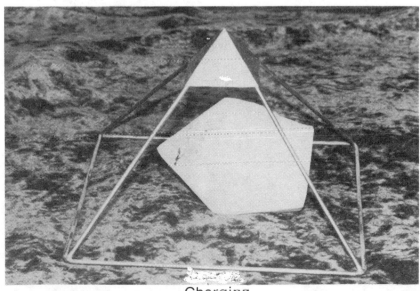

Charging

CHARGING

It was mentioned earlier about charging a crystal with different energy systems such as pyramids and orgone accumulators. They can also be charged with the focused energy of a group. Here are two exercises to work with:

Form a group of three or more in a circle with the crystal in the center. Hold hands and close your eyes. Each person visualize sending a beam of light from his heart to the heart of the person on his left. Send another beam of light around the back of the person on your right. You now have two concentric moving circles of light, one moving clockwise in the center and the second moving counter-clockwise on the outside. With these circles of light moving faster and faster, imagine sending a beam of light from each person's forehead into the crystal in the center. See that light create a swirling column of energy until it engulfs and creates one brightly glowing crystal.

The diameter of the field created in this crystal can be measured by a pendulum, a dowsing rod or a Cameron Aurameter.

Exercise number two:

Form a circle around the crystals you want to charge. Put your personal crystal in your right hand. With your left hand grasp the right wrist of the person on your left. The circle should be completely linked with hands resting on right wrists. Point your personal crystals toward the center where the other crystals are waiting to be charged. This will be more comfortable if you do it seated. One half-hour is the recommended charging time. Measure the energy in any of the suggested methods. The energy gain of these crystals can be photographed, using a Kirlian camera.

Charging - Exercise One

Charging - Exercise Two

Practical Applications

BETTER GAS MILEAGE

Charged crystals are excellent for placing on your fuel line for extended gasoline mileage. Select a crystal from two to three inches long and charge in a pyramid or by one of the other methods. Attach it with metal hose clamps to the intake gasoline line four inches from the carburetor with the point of the crystal facing the carburetor. Check your average mileage prior to the crystal placement. After the crystal is attached, check it again. Our experience shows a ten to twenty percent increase in mileage.

INCREASE ELECTRICAL EFFICIENCY

To increase the efficiency of your refrigerator, take a three- to four-inch diameter clear cluster of crystals which has been charged by any of the aforementioned methods. Place the cluster on a shelf in the refrigerator. Within a week you should note an increase in its cooling ability. The refrigerator adjustment control usually does not need to be set past number two. In fact, several people reported it worked so well it froze food in the refrigerated area. This should make for a nice savings on your electric bill.

Pyramids & Crystals

The shape of the Great Pyramid of Egypt has unusual effects. The pyramid has a square base. The side angle from the base to the peak is approximately 52°. This form, when aligned to magnetic north, can cause unusual effects.

It can charge water so plants given the water grow faster and better. It can dry meat without decay, sharpen razors and change the taste of fruit and liquids. Quartz crystals grow in a spiral equal to the same angle, 52°. Quartz has many of the same properties plus all of the other piezoelectric abilities.

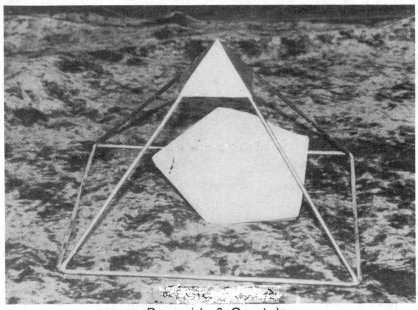

Pyramids & Crystals

Consciousness

For our purposes let us call consciousness a degree of awareness. By awareness we mean perception and understanding. Consciousness is a function of the mind. The mind is not the brain but is an energy field which uses the brain. How can a quartz crystal affect consciousness? The precise ordered structure of the molecules or lattice of a crystal, along with the fact that it grows in a spiral of the same degree as the side angle of the Great Pyramid, approximately 52°, activates the piezoelectric effect to change energy (the ability to amplify, store, transform, focus and transfer energy has been described previously). Because of this molecular precision, any energy entering the crystal will become precise or harmonized and balanced.

Thoughts are energy forms. When thought energy interacts with a crystal, those thoughts become modulated, changed to more harmonic forms. The harmony of thought patterns will cause a change in brainwave frequencies which are some indication of levels of consciousness. Any change in the patterns shows a possible change or alteration in consciousness.

We have noted an increase in alpha brain waves after holding a crystal for half an hour. Over a longer period of time there is an increase in theta and delta.

There are four major accepted brain wave patterns which seem to have connective links to levels of consciousness. **BETA**, or conscious mind level, starts at 14 cycles per second, measured on an electroencephalograph or EEG, and usually average about 21 cycles per second. **ALPHA** brackets from seven to 14 cycles per second and is called the dream or creative state, with light extra sensory perception, cell energy renewal and first level of suggestibility for the subconscious mind. **THETA** is from four to seven cps and is deeper states of ESP and beginning level for psychokinesis or PK, painless surgery and dentistry, and very powerful levels of suggestibility. **DELTA** is from one-half to four cycles per second. It is known as deep sleep. In delta all the ESP and PK talents work, it is the level of total recall and total suggestibility, the level of non-resistance.

Research is continuing with our crystal groups with using crystals to understand and control all of these states of mind. We expect dramatic breakthroughs in the fields of theta and delta.

Programming

The subconscious mind is the controller of the physical body and affects the mind and emotions through its ability to store thoughts and emotional programs which operate automatically when given the right stimulus. These programs govern much of what we do and how think.

The language of the subconscious mind is symbols. All information is stored in the subconscious mind in the form of pictures coupled with emotional motivators. Say a word out loud like "apple." For a moment the picture of an apple flashed into your mind as your brain converted the sound of the word into a picture and stored it. By using pictures you gain access into the computer-like functions of the subconscious and give it new commands.

The crystal stimulates the energy centers in the center of the forehead and the top of the head. These in turn stimulate the clairvoyant ability, making internal visualizing easier. A picture can now be held in the mind more easily and given a greater push into the inner consciousness.

To change a program or pattern, think about the old pattern. Hold the crystal in your left hand and picture the pattern changing into the way you want it. Hold that picture clearly and surround it with sparkling light. After the first time, only visualize the final change and surround it with sparkling light. Do not recreate the old image. Do this twice a day, once in the morning and once at night for 33 days. You should be able to change any pattern or habit within 33 days.

Do you want to change your weight? Picture yourself stepping on the scales and seeing your present weight.

Actually do this and then recreate it in your mind. Picture using a crystal like a laser beam to melt off the extra weight and sculpt the exact shape you want. With your new shape mentally see yourself stepping back on the scales and weighing the exact amount you want. Surround the image with sparkling light. Repeat the process twice a day for 33 days. Remember, after the first time, each repetition visualizes only the finished result, the new change. Do not recreate the picture!

Think of it as accessing into a computer. You picture the

situation as it is stored now in the memory banks. This is the key to getting into the area where the program is stored. Now, visualize and create the change. It helps to become emotional about the change. If you really want to change, put that desire in with your picture. You do not recreate the original picture because you may reactivate the old program and wipe out the change you made. Instead, only picture the new program. Each repeat will reinforce the change until your computer accepts the change and creates a new reality for you. Visualizing can work on habits, talents, abilities and the physical body. It is the basis for most healing.

Spiritual Guides

All of us have spiritual guides and teachers. Sometimes they are called guardian angels. They are the little voices which warn you of danger and whisper answers to your problems. They are what cause you to go to a bookstore, pick a book out at random, open it and find yourself reading a page describing the information you have been looking for. They are the ones you see in your dreams, the last voices you hear before you awaken. Their job is to guide you and assist you in making correct decisions about your life. You can consciously communicate with them. You can ask questions and get answers. The more you use them the better the results.

Sit down in a comfortable position, feet flat on the floor. Place your crystal in your left hand and close your eyes. See the crystal with the point up. Come in closer. As you get closer, the crystal gets larger until it is as big as a house. There is an open door. Go inside and look around. Light is coming down from the ceiling reflecting on the walls and floor. What do the walls look like? How do you see the floor? Feel the temperature. Smell the odor of the inside of the crystal. Listen to the sounds of the crystal. Feel the walls and floor. What do these surfaces feel like? Establish the sensory reality of the inside of the crystal. Walk over to the center where your chair sits. Look at it. How is it designed? What fabrics and materials are used? Sit down on it. This is the most comfortable chair you will ever know. In front of you are two more chairs. A man and a woman walk in and sit down on the chairs.

Look first at the man. What color is his hair? How old would you say he is? What kind of clothing does he have on? Does he have a beard or is he clean-shaven? What is his name? Now look at the woman. How old is she? What color is her hair? What type of clothing is she wearing? What is her name? These are two of your spiritual guides. They have much to tell you. Be still and listen to their message.

When the message is complete, give them a hug and step out of the crystal and back into your body. When you feel comfortable, open your eyes.

If at first you do not feel much was communicated, keep trying. Practice will improve the connection. Try simple questions at first, gradually getting more complex as you gain confidence. Remember this: A Spiritual Guide always works to help you help yourself, they never give orders — only suggestions. You must make your own decisions.

Manifesting

Manifesting is a method of programming the subconscious mind to create something in your life you want or need. Certain things are needed for your manifestation to come into reality. First, you must know what you want, since fuzzy or incomplete thoughts will manifest very little. If you want a new car, know the model, the year, the color, the accessories — everything you want. If you want a talent or ability, be sure you know exactly what it is.

When you're sure you know what you want, follow this simple procedure:

Get in a comfortable position. Hold your crystal in your left hand. Close your eyes. See your crystal in front of you with the point up. See it getting larger and larger until it is as large as a house. There is a door open. Go inside. Once again, look around you. Look at the light coming through the ceiling and shining on the walls and floor. Smell the odor of the crystal. Listen to the special sound. Taste the crystal. Feel the temperature. Touch the walls and feel the surface.

Walk over to the doorway which says "Manifesting Room." Walk into the room and look around. The walls are solid gold. The floor is green. The ceiling is studded with millions of precious gemstones, sparkling with all the colors of the rainbow. The room is filled with a warm feeling of total prosperity.

If you are manifesting a new car, bring the image of the car into the manifesting room. Look at it carefully and see that it is the right color, interior, model and make. Be sure it has all the right accessories such as radio, air conditioning, stereo cassette, sun roof, coffee maker, sauna, hot tub, pool, or whatever you want.

Open the door and sit down in the driver's seat. Feel the cushions settle, put your feet on the pedals, check the lights, blow the horn and smell the new smell inside. Let all your senses be aware of the whole car. Now, reach inside the glove compartment and pull out the receipt with your name on it marked PAID IN FULL. Take the receipt, put it in your pocket and say out loud, "This is mine; I own it; it belongs to me." Say this three times with as much feeling and acceptance as you can. End the manifesting with the statement, "In all I create, let Divinity be my guide." Now, come out of the manifesting room, step out of your crystal and back into your body. When you feel comfortable, open your eyes.

Do this twice a day for 33 days.

If you want to manifest for a talent, choose the talent carefully. Do you want to be a painter? an artist? What type of painting do you most admire?

Get in a comfortable position. Hold your crystal in your left hand. Close your eyes and see the crystal in front of you getting as big as a house. Go inside. Walk down to the Manifesting Room and go inside. Bring in the artists you admire and have them show you how to paint. Create your own painting inside your crystal. Come out of the crystal and transfer what you know to canvas.

Manifesting for a musical talent is the same. Ask for the Master to teach you. Practice in your crystal and then practice with your body and the physical instrument.

If you want to manifest a companion, remember to be careful for you will get exactly what you ask for. Know what you want. Always ask for that companion who will be the right one for you.

At one of my counseling sessions a lady asked me if I could teach her to program to get rid of someone. This was certainly different from most requests I get, since most people want to manifest someone into their lives. She wanted to manifest someone out of hers. When I questioned her, she admitted she had attended a prosperity seminar from another teacher and learned how to manifest. She wanted a companion, but not just any companion. She wanted the perfect man. She did the manifesting and sure enough, she got him. He was handsome, athletic, well read, intelligent and owned his own successful business. He played music like a professional and wrote both music and poetry. He was both sensitive and assertive. He even owned his own home. He adored her. He took her everywhere and showered her with gifts.

She was miserable. She could hardly stand to be around him. He was perfect, all right, but she was not. She was frantic with all the effort it took to keep up with him.

So she asked me to help her to get rid of him. I suggested we do so in a way which would benefit him and ease the blow. I suggested she help to manifest the **perfect girl for him.**

Several months later I met her at a party and when I questioned her, she glumly admitted her former boy friend had met someone else and they were married. She was a little piqued at how quickly he fell in love with someone else. We laughed together and I suggested she manifest once again for herself. She was a little reluctant to do so after the results of her first attempt. This time I suggested she manifest for the **perfect man for her,** one who would more perfectly complement her own imperfection. She agreed to do so and as far as I know they are still living together.

As we said, there are a few simple rules for manifesting. Always invoke the Light, "I invoke the Light of Christ within me. I am a clear and perfect channel. Light is my guide." Leave the method for manifestation open. The Universe knows more ways to achieve than you do. Be prepared to take action of your own to complete it. It may come as an opportunity to earn it. It may also come as a complete gift.

One of our graduates manifested $10,000 in the form of a cashier's check with no strings attached. Another manifested a special job which paid her exactly what she requested.

These are actual examples of how it works. Try it. You'll be amazed at the results.

Prosperity Consciousness

If you are interested in always having what you want and need, you may develop a way of being which attracts everything to you. We call this Prosperity Consciousness. The steps to achieving prosperity consciousness are exact and simple. There are five steps.

One: Write out this phrase, "I have everything I need to do the things I want and I have everything I want to do the things I need." Do this 100 times. Separate each phrase so they can be cut into 100 pieces, each having the full statement on it.

Two: Cut them into pieces and tape them everywhere your eyes can see them, on the doors, walls, refrigerator, toilet, mirrors, ceilings, light fixtures, car dash, work desk, any and everywhere your eyes look.

Three: Take a sixty minute cassette tape. Record on one side the phrase: "I have everything I want to do the things I need and I have everything I need to do the things I want." Repeat the phrase over and over again with as much feeling as possible for the full thirty minutes of tape on one side.

Four: Play the tape recording every night at very low volume just before falling asleep. Use a recorder that will shut off automatically when the tape is finished.

Five: Each morning after dressing but before breakfast, repeat the affirmation three times in front of a mirror with as much feeling as you can put into it. "I have everything I need to do the thing I want and I have everything I want to do the things I need."

Continue playing your tape at night and repeating your affirmations in the morning for 33 days for Total Prosperity Consciousness.

The Prosperity Consciousness techniques can be used concurrently with your manifesting. Do the manifesting after you do your prosperity affirmations. Remember, when you manifest you must be specific and precise. Always, before manifesting, invoke the Light: "I invoke the Light of Christ within. I am a clear and perfect channel. Light is my guide." What you want must be as exact as you can make it. If you want clothes, be sure they are the style, color and fit for you. If you want money, specify the exact amount you need, see each bill, and put some feeling behind the request. If it is a companion, define the qualities you want and request compatibility with you.

You will get what you ask for. Finish your manifestation with this statement: "In all that I create, let Divinity be my guide."

Psychic Ability

One question keeps recurring: Can crystals give you psychic abilities? The answer is yes — and no. You already have them built in, no one and nothing can or needs to give them to you. Crystals **can** stimulate these abilities and enable you to access into them, if that is what you desire.

We recommend finding one or more teachers you are comfortable with. You can choose among thousands of teachers and systems to help you develop your psychic abilities.

Choose your teacher with care. Check the abilities of his students as a measure of his teaching ability. Choose a teacher who will show you how to use your psychic talents to help others. If you hold a crystal while you are training, it will be easier and go faster. One suggestion I can make: Learn to use your healing abilities. This type of service is the fastest and safest way known to develop all your intuitive abilities. One valuable tool for healing is clairvoyance, or inner-vision.

Visualization, an important part of the mental crystal technique, is a function of clairvoyance. Clairvoyance is a natural function of our senses — it is the inner sense which corresponds to the outer sense of sight (our other outer senses — hearing, smell, taste and touch — also have corresponding inner senses).

Clairvoyance is defined as "clear seeing." Any improvement in this ability will be beneficial.

A powerful clairvoyant sense makes inner pictures sharp and clear. Simply going into the crystal and seeing the walls, floors and rooms as often as possible will exercise this ability. Practice will increase the sharpness of your perception.

Here are four exercises which will help you.

Light a candle and place a clear crystal or a crystal ball in front of the candle. Watch the candle flame through the crystal for three minutes. Close your eyes. Watch the after-image of the candle and keep it in front of you as long as you can. If the image disappears, open your eyes and stare at the candle again for three minutes. Close your eyes and hold the flame image in view. Try to hold it longer each time. Do this for thirty minutes each night in a darkened room.

Crystal Candle Gazing

Another method is to tape a clear, amethyst or lapis quartz piece over your brow, between your eyes and up one inch, while you meditate, pray or sleep. An elastic band will also keep it in place. The piece may be any shape, including the natural. Tumbled polished pieces seem to be most effective. In other cultures a slit is sometimes made in the skin in that area and a small crystal is inserted. The skin is then sewn shut.

A third exercise is to place a piece of clear, amethyst or lapis quartz on the forehead and sit in front of a mirror. Focus your attention on the stone on the forehead and observe it for thirty minutes. Imagine waves of light pulsing from the stone. Do not be frightened if you begin to observe your face changing. This is a common phenomenon. You may grow a beard or mustache, or have a male or female face. Some people think these are the faces of past lives. Whether they are or not, they are interesting to watch.

One other way is to stare into a fixed point in a crystal ball for thirty minutes a day. After a period of time, you may begin to see images in the ball. This is a function of your clairvoyance.

Meditation & Prayer

Meditation is the process of disconnecting the outer senses to enable the inner senses to be perceived. For us to function as unified beings, we need to be balanced and complete. Our inner consciousness structures our reality according to the data it receives from the outer and the inner senses.

We exercise the outer senses far out of proportion to the inner senses. Meditation serves to equalize that proportion. When we achieve a proper balance between the inner and outer senses, we may attain a harmony in mind and body. If you have a structured system of meditation, continue it, but hold a crystal in your left hand. You may also place a crystal, upright, in front of you. If you have no method, here are some simple ones:

Meditation number one: In a darkened room, place a crystal upright in front of you with a lit candle behind it. Place it at eye level. As you observe the candle flame as seen through the crystal, be aware of your breathing, of how breath goes in and out of your body. Continue to observe the flame and be aware of your breathing. You may find your attention wandering and thoughts coming into your mind. Allow them to come and go. Continue to see the flame and be aware of your breathing. If you find your thoughts taking the place of the exercise, gently bring your attention back to the breathing and the candle flame. Do this once a day for thirty minutes.

Meditation number two: Sit in a comfortable straight-back chair with your shoes off and feet flat on the floor. With your crystal in your left hand and the point facing toward you, close your eyes and repeat over and over again: "I am the Light of God." Do this for thirty minutes at least once a day.

Meditation number three: Repeat number two and use the Siddah Yoga mantra: "Om Namah Shivaya" which is pronounced **Ohm** Nah **Mah** Shee **Vah** Yah.

When praying, crystals promote greater clarity of thinking. Prayer is speaking to God through your mind and heart. Pray with a crystal and watch the difference.

Crystals & Religion

Crystals have been used in religious practices for thousands of years. Crystals have been consistently found in the tombs of priests and royalty in almost every archaeological dig.

Crystals, especially members of the quartz family, are referred to over 1700 times in the Christian Bible. Amethyst quartz was mentioned as the twelfth stone placed in the foundation of New Jerusalem, Revelations 21:19, 20, Authorized Version. It was the ninth stone on the breastplate of Aaron, the Hebrew High Priest, Exodus 28:18, Authorized Version.

The Roman and Eastern Orthodox Catholic churches use an amethyst quartz as a symbol of spiritual power. It is given to every bishop.

The Eastern Orthodox Catholic churches use gems and crystals in the Eucharist and the building of the altar of the Seven Rays, when they invoke seven archangels to fill their altar.

When you look at the design and growth of crystals you can see the hand of Divinity. Their perfection and beauty are all signs of God's handiwork. All of the marvelous properties God gave the crystals are available for you to use to help your fellow man. You must choose whether you will take this opportunity to serve.

Communication

We have written earlier about the use of crystals in communication devices. Loudspeakers, radios, television sets and telephones all use crystals to send and receive information. Crystals are also valuable for inner or internal communication.

Telepathy is a form of communication similar to radio. The crown chakra at the top of the head receives and broadcasts thoughts as pictures and feelings. If you want some type of structure, consider thought pictures as nouns and your emotions as verbs. The pictures are the form and content of your thoughts. Here is a fun exercise:

Two people each take a crystal. Now each of you hold your crystal in your left hand. Take off your shoes and put your feet flat on the floor. Decide which person will be the sender and which will be the receiver. Both of you close your eyes. Picture the ocean with waves tossing and breaking. Hear the sound of the waves, sense the smell of the sea air and the taste of salt water on your lips. Watch the waves calm down until they become completely still, as smooth as glass, the whole ocean a giant, smooth, shiny mirror. Let the sender now create an object on the mirror — a fish, ship, bird, or anything else. The receiver simply observes and records what he sees. Do this for three minutes. The sender interacts with the images and fills them with his emotions. The receiver records everything. After three minutes, compare notes. Then reverse positions and let the sender become the receiver.

Try other variations. Send an emotion. See if the receiver can feel your emotion accurately. Create a sound in your mind and see if the receiver can pick it up. Make up a smell or taste and see if they can be transferred. It can be a great game.

Other intelligences are already communicating by telepathy. The crystal can get you in touch with them. You can contact spiritual guides, ascended masters, teachers, great personalities of the past, angels and space people.

How much of what you receive is real and how much is illusion? You have to decide. If you receive advice or information which can be used beneficially, it is good. If the advice or information cannot be used, or if "it" tries to control you with statements of "you should, ought, or must," then ignore it.

Telepathy

If you want your information to be consistently usable, here is a simple routine to do before using the crystal. Hold it in your left hand and mentally or verbally say: "I invoke the Light of Christ within me. I am a clear and perfect channel and Light is my guide." If you have a religious preference, you may substitute God for Christ. Christ won't mind.

A good way to start the communication process is to place a crystal in your left hand and ask questions that can be answered yes or no. Make them simple and clear and listen for the answer. You will get a yes or no. Sometimes you will get both: Yes-no, No-yes. Take the first response. Ask everyday items you can check. Will your friend be at home when you telephone? Call and see. Keep track of your accuracy, without judgment.

As you continue the exercise, you will get greater accuracy as you learn to listen and trust your responses. You can use it to choose your food, your clothes, and check if parking places are available. Once you establish a line of communication there is no limit to the uses of the crystal.

As you master the technique you will find yourself using it more frequently, for you seem to have greater accuracy than when you just use your logical mind.

Intuition & Creativity

When working with crystals, one effect seems universal. Intuition begins to show itself. This can be either illuminating or upsetting, depending on you. It could be upsetting to know who is on the other end when the phone rings, or it can be delightful. For me, it became a source of wonder and curiosity. Were my experiences real? How could they be? If they were, how did they operate? How **did** crystals fit in?

I knew these strange events increased when I held a crystal or kept one with me. Over a period of time constant exposure wore down my skepticism. I went from "Does it work?" to "How does it work?" From my observations I noted two things operating — feelings and thoughts. That seemed to be the sequence of the pattern: first feelings, then thought. I observed the ability of the crystal to amplify energy and even photographed the effect using a Kirlian camera. I reasoned the crystal must amplify mental and emotional energy in such a way as to give me access into these intuitive levels. I also noticed I had more experiences of greater intensity when I held the crystal in my left hand. Then I realized the left side of my body corresponded to the right hemisphere of my brain, where intuitive activity seems to be connected. I coupled that with meditating with a crystal and doing the simple yes-no exercise previously mentioned. All of these accelerated the process of opening latent intuitive levels. I was not trying to develop psychic powers. I just wanted to get in touch with that part of me that **knows** without having to **reason.**

My conclusion was that I do not fully know how the crystal activates intuition but that working with a crystal, even just having one, will open up that creative flow and help you become more creative.

Creativity seems to be an activity of intuition. My experience has shown both function when either is stimulated. If you want to be creative, it is simple. All you need to do is to begin to create. Does this seem too simple? A professional writer once told me the secret of writing. He said, "Begin writing." Want to paint? "Start painting." Technique is unimportant at first. As you begin any creative effort, you will attract to you or be attracted to techniques.

One important rule: **SUSPEND JUDGMENT**. Every effort you make creatively is unique and should never be compared to anything else. Grandma Moses was not much for technique but her work was unique. I will tell you a secret. She did not paint for the approval of others, she did it for herself.

Direct your creativity to express your feelings. Technique will come with practice. If you wear a crystal or keep one with you, your creative flow can come alive. When you feel this movement, let it out. Do something with it. Allow it to express. You will be amply rewarded.

Energy Measuring Tools

The crystal itself is a tool. It is one of the most viable tools we have because it links and works with the mind. All of our body is a system of crystals which channel energies and convert them into whatever the body needs. Examine dried blood on a slide and you will see crystals. Blow your breath on glass and examine it with an electron microscope. You will see crystals. Even the DNA and RNA are resonating crystals.

The mind is the master director and controller of all these resonating crystals which make up the giant liquid crystals of our bodies. With that knowledge it can be understood that there are some ways to combine and arrange crystals and other materials to create definitive effects.

We have mentioned several ways to measure the energy fields of the crystal. Few of these are scientific. They would not please a laboratory physicist, but they do indicate an energy field is present and give us some suggestion of the relative size of the field. This allows us to experiment with different combinations and methods. Some of the simple tools we use are:

PENDULUM. The pendulum is a device for getting information from the inner self using some type of material suspended from a chain or a piece of string. Almost any material with some weight will do. The very best and most responsive pendulum uses a crystal.

Take a quartz crystal and glue a bell cap on the end of it, opposite the point, or tie a loop around the end and tie a length of string or thread so the crystal will dangle from the end. It is best if the crystal is balanced so the point hangs down. Hold the string at a point three to four inches from the crystal and let the crystal dangle. Focus your attention on the crystal pendulum and mentally direct it to move forward and back. When this occurs, direct it to move side to side, then in a clockwise circle and last in a counter-clockwise circle. When the pendulum moves satisfactorily, mentally direct the pendulum to begin moving when it detects an energy field. Step away from the center of the energy field. Hold the pendulum in front of you and walk slowly toward the center of the field. A little practice will make you quite sensitive and accurate.

There are several good books on pendulums. We recommend "Pendulum Power" by Polanski and Nielson and, for fun, "Stalking the Wild Pendulum" by Itzak Bentof.

DOWSING RODS. Take two wire coat hangers and bend them into a straight line. Cut off and discard the curled ends and bend each wire 90º at about one-third of the way from the end. When you have both bent, hold them in your hands by the short end so the long ends point in front of you and are level to the ground.

Mentally direct the dowsing rods to move when they detect an energy field. Take care to hold them lightly enough that they may turn freely in your fingers. Walk toward the energy with both rods pointing forward. When they reach the edge of the energy field, the rods will either cross or turn out.

THE CAMERON AURAMETER. Designed by master dowser Vern Cameron, this device consists of a three-inch flattened metal tube with a nine-inch length of piano wire attached to one end. The wire goes straight away from the tube for about two inches and then has six coils wound counter-clockwise. The wire goes straight out for another six inches and has a two-inch metal bar with a pointed tip attached to its end.

The Aurameter is held lightly with the thumb and forefingers gripping the larger metal tube. The pointed metal end is aimed toward the energy source. Mentally direct the Aurameter to respond when it detects an energy field. When it reaches the edge of the field, it will deflect away from it.

There are much more complex and expensive devices which can detect energy fields. There is a device invented by Dr. George Motoyama which measures the conductivity of the acupuncture energy meridians. This machine can measure changes in the energy systems of the physical body. It is an excellent tool for showing the changes which take place when healing is done with a crystal.

THE KIRLIAN CAMERA, named after Semyon Kirlian, who popularized the method. This is a method whereby Life Energy can be photographed.

The photography is done in a high voltage field of 50,000 volts or more, but with very low amperage. In this field subtle energies can clearly be seen which are not normally detectable. When photographed in color, they show different colors and shades. The camera can show differences in an individual's energy field both before and after using the crystals.

Take a photograph of the finger tips of the right hand prior to healing and then after healing and see if there is a difference in the energy fields. Another test is to photograph the finger tips and then immediately hold a crystal in the left hand and take a another picture. Observe the difference between the two photos.

Pendulum

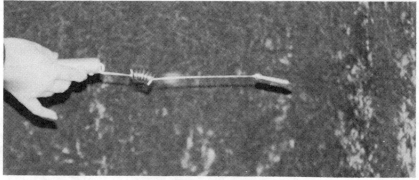

Cameron Aurameter

Synthetic Crystals

Crystals can be grown in a laboratory using a slice of natural crystal as a seed. This is placed in a tank with liquid and crushed natural crystal and exposed to pressure and an electrical current. Synthetic crystals can be grown in days while it could take an equivalent natural crystal thousands of years to grow. There is a difference. The natural crystal may have taken thousands of years to grow, but during those years it absorbed all of the energies of the earth changes. These energies give the natural crystal abilities and information the synthetic ones do not have.

Consider the synthetic to be a clone, artifically reproduced from the real thing. It is like a baby with no grooves in the brain. It has no intelligence and no information. It operates only on stimulus and response. It will function on the beginning energy levels but not on the higher levels. Synthetics could be used to send energy on the second energy level, the electric sheath directly around the physical body. It would not be able to work on the emotional or higher mental levels.

Science has discovered the synthetics are limited as compared to natural crystals. In a computer memory, the synthetics begin to lose their information storage abilities after several years. The natural ones never lose that ability.

Synthetics can be transformed into naturals by several methods. One way is to place a synthetic crystal next to a natural crystal under a pyramid for 33 days. Another method requires mentally projecting into the synthetic crystal to create seven doorways for the seven masters of the seven rays. Ask the masters to come forth and teach the crystal. It takes seven days.

Jewelry

An excellent way to keep energized with a crystal is to wear it as a piece of jewelry. It not only is decorative but will work on your energy systems as long as it is worn.

Several styles can be worn. If you desire a focus of energy on the throat chakra, wear a **necklace.** Be sure the stones are natural and the metals are compatible. The best metals are copper, silver and gold. Other lesser metals would be nickel, titanium, platinum, iron and steel. Aluminum is very poor and should be avoided.

When **pendants** are worn, they should rest over the heart chakra. For most people this means using an 18 to 20 inch chain. This stimulates the thymus gland which controls the immune system of the body to keep you healthier. If a natural pendant is used, it can be worn with the point either up or down. If it is pointed up it will stimulate the upper chakras. It might be beneficial to wear this type when meditating or channeling. It is not recommended for normal wear because it stimulates out-of-body experience, tending to make you "spacey." When worn with the point down there is a grounding effect, keeping you more down-to-earth, in your body and capable of handling your everyday affairs. Both types will amplify your body energy. The point of the crystal merely directs the flow of energy.

Earrings help to balance the left and right hemispheres of the brain. They also help to stabilize the throat chakras.

When wearing **rings,** be sure the underside of the stone of the ring is open to allow free access from the crystal to the skin.

All jewelry should be cleansed by washing in soap and water and putting the pieces in sea salt for seven days.

A salt solution may be used, if you prefer, by dissolving a half-pound of salt in a gallon of water. All jewelry either personally purchased or received as gifts should be cleansed to remove other people's vibrations.

Protection

There are many crystals which can be used for psychic protection. Simply keeping one in your pocket or wearing it around your neck will increase the strength of the energy fields outside your physical body. This is your shield or force field which will stop most negative or imbalanced thoughts and emotions.

To increase or strengthen that field, use the following technique:

Hold your crystal in your left hand and close your eyes. Mentally look down at your waist and picture your aura as a white band of energy around the waist. Expand your aura out about a foot. See that white band get brighter and begin to clear until it is completely clear like a crystal ball all around you. Any negative emotion, like a dark arrow, which strikes that shield will change to a white arrow of positive energy which can be used for yourself or sent to others.

Use this technique every morning to armor yourself against the emotional turmoil of the rest of the world.

For additional spiritual protection, use the Light Invocation: "I invoke the Light of Christ within me. I am a clear and perfect channel. Light is my guide."

Another technique:

Hold your crystal in your left hand and close your eyes. Picture a ball of light in the center of your chest. See the light begin to spin and get larger. It gets larger and larger until it fills your body and expands outward. As the light expands, all darkness will go before it. Expand the light until it is about a foot away from your body.

The best defense is a loving offense. If you feel someone is draining your energy, either deliberately or not, channel Divine Light and send it to that person. See him filled with light, shining and glowing like a beacon.

Amulets & Talismen

An amulet is a stone designed to be worn for protection. It may be inscribed with a design or be part of a design.

A talisman is a stone which has some type of design incorporated in it for the purpose of assisting in some ritual or ceremony. It is used to amplify, channel or cause some catalytic process to take place.

Any crystal can be an amulet. A quartz crystal automatically amplifies the auric energy fields of the body. This extra strength is our first line defense against the imbalanced or negative thoughts of others. If you program your crystal, you can direct your mind to change any imbalanced energy to become balanced by the time your sense perceptors receive it. This technique is incorporated into the section on clearing. It will strengthen your auric field. Any energy coming into your body must come through this field.

You can couple this with the Light Invocation. "I invoke the Light of Christ within me. I am a clear and perfect channel. Light is my guide." This will create a strengthening in your etheric body which will shield you from curses and spells. If you have a special saint or spiritual master, call upon him to fill you with his presence. If you are holding your crystal while doing all of this, you will impart these desires and wishes as commands. They will automatically protect you against others who may wish you ill.

These amulets can be further empowered by enscribing the stones or making the stones part of a special design which may give it additional power. Some examples would be a cross, heart, five-pointed star, six-pointed star, Egyptian ankh, or a picture of a master, angel, saint or other spiritual teacher.

Crystals as talismen are usually part of a larger object.

Wands are talismen. Crystals can be embedded in the shaft of the wand or on the tip. Some wands have different types of gems set into the sides in a particular pattern. As with all talismen, wands are designed to cause a change in someone or something. This means manipulating energy, since everything is energy.

A simple wand can be made with a crystal stuck into the end of a piece of copper tubing.

A very special wand can be made for healers, using a piece of olive wood, 3/4-inch thick and seven inches long, with a 1/8-inch hole drilled through the center of the wand from the tip to the other end. To enable crystals to be set in each end, center drill each end 1/2 inch down with a 1/2-inch drill.

Two crystals are needed — a clear natural quartz crystal and a natural amethyst. The back of the clear quartz and the tip of the amethyst should be drilled to a depth of 1/4 inch, using a drill bit one size larger than a seven-inch piece of 22-gauge 14K gold wire. The back of the amethyst should be ground into a dome shape and polished clear. Both crystals should be large enough to fit snugly into the 1/2-inch sockets at either end of the wand. Using mucilage or some other natural glue, attach the gold wire into the drilled end of the clear crystal and set the crystal into one end of the wand with the gold wire inserted into the length of the wand. Put the other end of the gold wire into the drilled tip of the amethyst and set the amethyst into the other end of the wand. You now have an etheric surgery device for spiritual healing.

A wizard's staff can be made with crystals and is usually as large as a walking stick.

Education

Education should be the process of gaining knowledge. Most educational systems are satisfied if their students can memorize large amounts of often outdated information. Only a few offer actual experience to make the data real. Nevertheless, we have the system and must make the most of it.

Working with a crystal offers several benefits to a student. The crystal's ability to harmonize emotions creates the calmness necessary for clear thinking. The Hall of Knowledge offers an endless wealth of information. Your spiritual guides can help. Use of the Brain Crystal technique will stimulate all mental activity. Persistent use of the memory method will aid in improving recall of data.

Another technique is very helpful for someone taking a test, and is especially good for children who are terrified of tests. When taking a test, answer all the questions you know. Then close your eyes and go inside your crystal, bringing the image of the teacher into the crystal with you. Ask the teacher the answers to the questions you don't know. Your teacher will tell you.

One crystal graduate is now pursuing her master's degree at the University of California at Berkeley. She uses this technique and and is getting straight A's.

Hall of Knowledge

Within crystals are many corridors into many dimensions of the mind. For seekers of the wisdom of the ages we offer this doorway:

Get into a comfortable position with your crystal in your left hand. Close your eyes. Picture your crystal in front of you getting larger and larger until it is the size of a house. Go inside. Walk down the corridor to the doorway marked Hall of Knowledge. Walk inside and look around. This is a vast library with rows and rows of crystals on shelves instead of books. In these crystals is all the knowledge of the universe.

Any subject you desire can be yours. Think of the subject and that crystal will begin to flash off and on. Pick up the crystal and hold it in your hands. In front of you, as if on a large screen, will appear the information from the crystal. You will have full sensory awareness of the data, just as though you were actually there. When you are finished with your knowledge crystal, return it to the shelf.

Keep a tape recorder on and, if you can, keep up a running description of what's occurring. If not, recall all you can afterward. Some people have described this as the Akashic Records.

Brain Crystals

Here is a nice technique for stimulating the brain:

Get into a comfortable position with your crystal in your left hand. Close your eyes. Picture your crystal with the point up, getting larger and larger until it is as large as a house. Go inside. Once again look around at the inside of the crystal. Look at the walls and floors and ceiling. What's the temperature like? Smell the inside of the crystal. Feel the surface of the walls.

When you have reestablished contact with the crystal, walk over and sit in your personal chair. Wave hello to your spiritual guides.

Look down at yourself sitting there. Come in more closely and look at your head. It has hinges on the back of the head. Look down inside and see the crystals in your brain. Some of the crystals are glowing. Some are very dim. Take a crystal from your pocket and cause a wide beam of light to come out of it like a crystal spotlight. Shine that light on every crystal in the brain until all the crystals are shining. Put a circle around the area of your memory.

To increase your memory, read or listen to the material you wish to recall. Go inside your brain and spray light on the crystals in the memory circle. Go back outside and read or listen to the material. Once again go inside your brain. Spray light on the memory section and see the crystals get brighter. A third time, go back out and read or listen and then return inside the brain and spray light on the memory area. See the crystals so bright it is difficult to look at them. Do this three times each day for 33 days.

How does your head feel? Is it pulsating with pressure? Good, you are growing!

Energy Bodies

When most people think of a body they mean the physical body. When we speak of the energy bodies we are describing different intensities of energies which operate together to power the human vehicle. The first body is the densest energy field and is the physical meat and bones.

The second would be the electrical and magnetic energy fields directly surrounding the physical body. These are called the etheric, the electrical, pranic, orgone, or emotional bodies. These energy fields act upon the physical body through the meridian points and the chakras.

Meridians are the interior energy lines of the body. The points are where the lines cross each other or come to the surface of the body. The external energy fields are called chakras, a Sanskrit term meaning "wheel." When photographed with a Kirlian camera they appear to be wheels of light. These chakras stimulate the endocrine glands which secrete hormones to regulate the chemical reactions for proper cell replacement and maintenance. The intensity and degree of balance of the emotions regulate the stimulation of the glands through the chakras. In other words, the way we feel directly affects the growth of the cells. Imbalanced emotions can cause imbalanced cellular growth.

The third energy frequency is the realm of thoughts, the mental body. Here we create thought forms which act upon the subconscious or inner conscious mind level. The subconscious mind controls all the energy processes of the body. Thought forms are one very strong way of affecting the subconscious to make changes in those energy processes. This is because most information is stored in the mind as symbols and they are moved into action by feelings.

Several things need to happen if you want a change to take place. First, the mind must be in the alpha brain wave level which is the entrance to the level of subconscious where suggestion can be made. The crystal causes a greater production of alpha whenever it is held. By visualizing, you then create a thought form. If you energize the thought form with an emotion, you can cause it to interact with the subconscious and cause changes in the energy field of the body.

ENERGY BODIES

Through the process of linking the crystal to visualization, you can direct the subconscious mind to move energy where you want it. First, you identify the problem with a symbolic picture and cause the picture to change. The mind will then bring about the change in energy.

Brain Crystals

Healing Stones

There are stones which work well on each of the energy bodies or levels. For the physical body, clear quartz, smoky quartz and green quartz are most effective.

Clear quartz is the overall body energizer. Smoky quartz is very good for grounding you into your body if you are having trouble paying attention to the world. Green quartz interacts with the endocrine glands to keep the body balanced. Pink rose quartz and citrine quartz work on the emotional body. The natural citrine, in the light orange to brown colors, balances the body emotions of the lower three chakras — the groin, splenic and solar plexus. The tumbled citrine in the golden color stimulates the crown chakra.

Rose quartz balances the love emotions of the upper four chakras — the heart, throat, brow and crown chakras. It is necessary for these four to be in balance for consciousness to be raised to the higher spiritual levels.

Lapis lazuli is a member of the quartz family. Its blue color is most effective for the mental body to promote clarity and depth of thought. In the natural state it can be used for protection for the body and in the tumbled state it works well for the area of the throat chakra.

Purple amethyst is the spiritual stone and changes or transmutes lower energies into higher frequencies of the spiritual levels.

Chakras

We have energy centers in the body called chakras. When the ancient clairvoyants looked at the energy centers, they saw them as spinning wheels of light, so they were called chakras, which in Sanskrit means "wheel."

There are seven major and five minor chakras. The seven major chakras are the root, spleen, solar plexus, heart, throat, brow and crown. The five minor chakras are the hands and feet and the hollow in the back of the head where the brain stem meets the spine, the Medulla Oblongata.

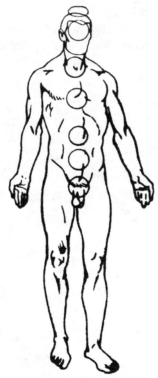

Chakras

The root chakra is located in the genital area. It interacts with the suprarenal cortex glands.

The spleen or second chakra is located between the genitals and the stomach about two inches below the navel. It stimulates the gonads.

The solar plexus is slightly above the navel and includes the stomach. The glands for the solar plexus chakra are the pancreas and the adrenals.

The heart chakra is in the center of the chest. This is the fourth chakra and it works with the thymus gland.

The fifth chakra is centered in the throat. It stimulates the thyroid gland.

The sixth chakra is often called the brow chakra and is centered in the forehead about an inch above the eyes. The corresponding gland is the pituitary.

The seventh chakra, located at the top of the head, is known as the crown chakra. It works in conjunction with the pineal gland. The combined interaction of the pineal and pituitary glands activates the Third Eye.

Here is a 6,000 year old technique, credited to the Sumerians, for balancing and energizing these chakras:

Get yourself in a comfortable position. Hold your crystal in your left hand. Close your eyes. See the crystal in front of you getting larger and larger until it is the size of a house. Go inside the open doorway. Once again, look around you. Look at the light and color beaming down from the ceiling. Look at the walls and floor. Smell the inside of the crystal. Listen to the sound. Taste a piece of crystal. Feel the surface of the walls and floor.

Walk down the corridor to the door marked "Healing Room." Step inside, over to the platform. Stand on the platform and turn around. As you look at your image on the platform you can see seven large circles of light on your body. These are your chakras, your energy centers.

Look at the first chakra, over your groin. Come in closer. As you move in closer, the opening becomes as large as a cave. Go on inside. As you look around you, the inside of the chakra looks like a cave with all the surfaces covered with crystals. Some of the crystals are glowing with light and some are very dim. Some of them have dark splotches of negative emotions.

Reach in your pocket and pull out a crystal. As you hold it, imagine a wide beam of light coming from the tip of the crystal like a floodlight.

Spray this wide beam of light energy over all of the crystals on the ceiling, walls and floor until every crystal begins to glow. Any dark bits of negativity will wash off and flow out the body's elimination system. Continue to spray light until you have all the crystals glowing and the whole interior filled with warm energy and perfectly balanced physically, emotionally and mentally.

Let the warm balanced energy lift you up, float you out of the first chakra and up into the second, halfway between the groin and the stomach.

Go inside and once again see all the crystals on the walls, ceiling and floor. Take out your crystal light and spray the ceiling, walls and floor. Light all the crystals and see the dark bits of negativity slide off and down the elimination system. When all the crystals are lit and glowing, let that warm, balanced energy lift you up and float you out of the second chakra into the third, the solar plexus, located just above but including the stomach.

Go into the opening and look around you. See the crystals on the ceiling, walls and floor. Spray the crystals with light and see all the dark bits of negativity slide down and out the elimination system. Continue to light up the crystals until every one is glowing in perfect balance, mentally, emotionally and physically.

Let the warm, balanced energy pick you up, float you out and up into the center of your chest, the fourth chakra, the heart. Once again, beam light on all the crystals throughout the area until every one is cleansed of the negativity and is glowing with warm energy.

Let that balanced energy lift you up and out and into the fifth chakra, the throat. Use your crystal spotlight and once again spray light on all the walls, ceiling and floor. Light up all the crystals. See the dark bits of negative emotions slide off the crystals and down the elimination system. When all the crystals are pulsing with a warm, balanced energy, let that warm energy pick you up, take you out and move you up into the center of the brow, the sixth chakra. Spray light onto every crystal in the floor, walls and ceiling until every crystal is filled with energy and all the dark bits of negative emotions are removed. In the back of the room is a large eye with a black tar-like substance covering the eyelid. Shine the crystal light on the eye. With the light, wash the black substance from the eyelid. When all the sticky matter has been washed away, open the eye. Watch the light shine out as a mighty beacon beaming through the brow as the Third Eye opens and begins to function. Feel that golden energy lift you up through a hole in the ceiling into a vast cavern, into the crown chakra, number seven.

In the center of the crown is a tremendous gemstone as large as house, with a thousand glistening facets. Some of the facets sparkle with light. Others are darkened. Shine your crystal spotlight on this gemstone as it slowly begins to revolve. Keep shining the light until every facet is glittering and bright. All of your talents and abilities, past, present or future, are now activated. They are waiting for you to use when they are needed. When all the facets are lit, feel the collective energies of all seven chakras begin to move upward in a rainbow of colors. Gold, red, orange, yellow, green, blue, purple and silver move out of the top of the head in a curved bow down to the bottom of the feet. The rainbow of colors moves up the feet, over the ankles, the calves, knees, thighs, over the hips and up the body. As it moves, the rainbow changes all the cells. They now vibrate with the full spectrum of rainbow color. Move that rainbow up the body over the shoulders and down the arms. Continue up the neck and out the top of the head in one continuous curving rainbow of energy down to the bottom of the feet and up the body. With that rainbow of energy still moving in you, step down from the platform, out of the Healing Room, out of the crystal and back into your body. When you feel comfortable, open your eyes.

Repeat this method as often as you wish. It will create dramatic changes in your emotional stability. The rainbow will open up higher spiritual talents and doorways. You can use this on others from a distance with noticeable results.

Healing

Using the crystal for healing is its most spectacular and controversial aspect. Much of this is because most people think of healing as mysterious, unusual, mystical or miraculous. The ability to beneficially affect the health of people without the traditional methods of modern medicine is seen as anything but normal. Only recently, and with great reluctance, have chiropractic and massage had limited acceptance with the medical community. Herbs are still viewed with suspicion and acupuncture is considered only a step away from witchcraft. All of these techniques have been used for centuries. Only lately has their use gained limited acceptance with traditional allopathic medicine. Much of the reluctance to accept new ideas has to do with the approach today's medicine has toward healing. Most doctors see patients only when their problems are severe, possibly life-threatening. The doctor's major concern is with the survival of the patient. He uses the most direct tools he has, surgery and drugs. By training, he looks upon disease and ill health as a problem of repairing the physical body and hoping, somehow, the body will rebuild itself. Unfortunately, surgery and drugs often have traumatic effects on that rebuilding process. At best they both have serious drawbacks. The miracle is the ability of the human body to repair itself anyway.

Modern medicine is late in accepting the fact of the total interrelationship of mind, emotions and body. People are not just chunks of meat and bone. They are thinking, feeling beings who interact constantly with their physical bodies. They cannot be separated from those bodies.

Crystal healing deals not with the physical body, but the energy systems which create and support that body. By logic alone we can see that the physical body is the end result of energy. Take energy away and what happens to the body? It breaks down. We get energy in many ways. Food is only one. We get it from water, from air and from the earth itself. Food is actually the least important. We can go without food for weeks, even months. We can live without water only a few days. And how long can you hold your breath?

Little is known about the way your body, in sleep, converts the electromagnetic field of the earth into the life energy the body can use. We do know we can't do without sleep. Deprived of it we deteriorate mentally, emotionally and physically.

The total human is a series of energy systems interconnecting the mind, emotions and body. Crystals can interact with these energy systems and in conjunction with the mind, create functional changes which will then manifest in the physical body.

Crystals have electronic piezoelectric properties. They can amplify, transform, store, transfer and focus energy. The human body is electronic in nature and responds to the crystal. If you hold a crystal in your left hand you will at least double the body energy field. Taking a picture of the fingers of the right hand using Kirlian photography will show this dramatic increase. Take a photograph of the right hand holding nothing. Put a crystal in your left hand and immediately take another photo of the right hand. The second photo will show a dramatic increase in the energy flowing from the finger tips. This ability to increase the energy field can be used for healing. You may be able to reduce pain this simple way:

Hold your crystal in your left hand. Place your right hand over the pain area. If the pain is on the right side, place the left hand with the crystal on the area, then grasp the left arm with the right hand. Hold these positions for half an hour.

If you watch television, do this while you watch your favorite half-hour show. You should have significant to total pain reduction with only a half-hour of this treatment. Does it sound too simple to be believed? It is simple.

The crystal amplifies energy. Energy flows in the left hand and out the right hand. If you place your right hand over the pain area you will decrease the pain by sending energy into that area. The nature of pain ensures this will happen.

Pain is not punishment, no matter what your memories tell you. Pain is a signal by the cells to the brain that something is wrong, which requires the brain to send energy to the cells so they can correct the problem. When the brain sends the energy the automatic repair system, which is built into every cell, begins the repair process. It will remove the dead cells and replace them with new ones. When the system becomes automatic and the cells do not need additional energy, the pain signal will shut off.

HEALING

The process of healing, when viewed as energy, becomes simple. When something blocks the flow of energy to the cells, the organs begin to die and you are sick. When energy is brought back to the area, new cells will form, rebuild the organs and you become well. In its simplest form, that's all there is to know about healing.

All the techniques of modern medicine are for the purpose of getting energy to the cells so they can repair themselves. No doctor or healer can really heal anyone except himself. All anyone can do for someone else is get energy to the cells so they will repair and heal themselves.

With the technique you just did, we use the amplifying ability of the quartz to give us this extra energy and we direct that energy to the area calling for it. This way we can speed up the healing process and reduce pain naturally rather than rely on pain killers.

Pain killers can interfere with the healing process. They coat the nerve endings so the signal from the cells never gets to the brain. The brain feels no pain, but since it does not know the cells are in trouble, it does not send the energy needed and the condition of the cells worsens. This is one reason why painful diseases are often debilitating. They progressively get worse. Arthritis is a good example.

With the crystal we feed energy to the cells instead of blocking the pain signal. The cells can now repair themselves and then turn off the pain because that signal is no longer needed. This is the natural healing way.

One particular pain problem is dealt with differently. Most pain needs energy for repair, but with a headache there is too much energy in the head. Energy flows in and out of the head all the time through the crown and brow chakras. When something, usually emotional, blocks the exit of the energy, it builds up pressure (like pinching the end of a water hose). The excess pressure causes the cells to signal the brain with pain. In this case we want to remove excess energy, not put in more.

Place the crystal in the right hand. Put your left hand on the the headache pain and the right hand over the solar plexus. Using the drawing ability of the left hand, amplified by the crystal in the right, we will now transfer the excess energy from the head to the solar plexus, where it can be redistributed throughout the body.

Releasing Headaches

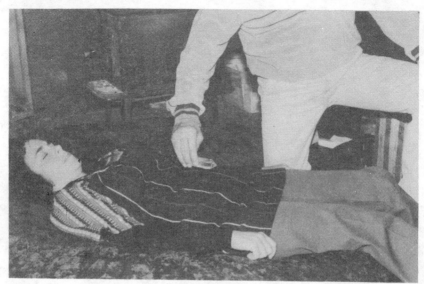

Scanning

This can take up to a half-hour to complete. To speed up the process, close your eyes and picture the headache as a dark cloud of excess energy. Your left hand is a giant vacuum cleaner and watch it suck the cloud away. Watch until the cloud is gone and then open your eyes. Put your hands down and stand up. Take a couple of deep breaths, walk around and wonder where the headache has gone.

These methods are not recommended for the treatment of cancer. They are not selective, and will send energy to the cancer cells as well as the normal ones. Cancer requires a more advanced method than is dealt with in this book.

Another healing practice is called the Aura Scan.

Have the client lie down on his back, hands beside him. Hold your crystal lightly between the thumb and the first three fingers. Start at the top of the head and hold the crystal about an inch away from the body at all times during this procedure. When you feel heat or a tingling sensation, begin to move the crystal slowly over the body. As you move, be aware of any change in the feel of the crystal or the body. The change may be a resistance to your movement, a sense of heat, a tingling sensation, coolness, or simply a feeling that something is there even if you have no sensation. When you come to such a change, stop and begin making a circular counter-clockwise motion around the center of the disturbance. Keep making this motion until you feel the crystal get heavier, pulling your hand down toward the body. Stop the circular motion and touch the tip of the crystal to the body in the center of the circle.

Continue to move the crystal down over the front and sides of the body. Wherever you find a difference, make a correction using the circular, counter-clockwise motion.

When you reach the feet and have finished, go back to the top of the head and move the crystal from the head to the feet in a sweeping motion. When doing this, imagine your client has feathers sticking out all over his body and you are smoothing down these feathers. This will align the auric energy pattern into a smooth, even movement.

HEALING

Turn the client over and do the back side, using the same procedure. Wherever you find a difference, stop and make a counterclockwise circular movement over that area. Once again, smooth down the feathers.

You have the chakras very open, now. Close them down to normal by imagining a zipper at the feet. Reach down and grasp the zipper and pull it all the way to the top of the head.

When you finish, your client will be very relaxed, even sleepy. The whole body will be in balance. In a short time the client should feel rested and stronger. Aches and pains and tension will lessen and there will be a sense of well being.

Where there are imbalances the cells will send out a signal to the brain for the brain to send enough energy for the cells to correct the problem. The strongest of these signals is pain. Any signal will be stronger than the rest of the energy field of the body, or it would not be a signal. You can detect this signal when your crystal passes over it because it is stronger. Making a counter-clockwise motion reduces the signal. When you feel the crystal getting heavier, you have equalized the signal with the field energy strength of the rest of the body. It is almost as though a magnet is pulling the crystal down to the body. When the entire body is equalized, no area is dominating and causing a disturbance in the distribution of energy within the body. With little or no resistance, the energy can flow more efficiently, making the overall body stronger.

We can show this increase by using an interesting technique called muscle testing or applied kinesiology. Have the client stand up and extend his right arm out, clench his fist and rotate it so the thumb is on the bottom. This affords the maximum tension on the arm. Press down on the fist as he resists you until you feel his arm begin to give, then stop. This will give you an idea of the amount of pressure you will use each time you test him. Let him rest his arm.

Now have him place the first three fingers of his left hand on each of the chakras, starting with the crown at the top of the head. As he touches each chakra with his left hand, test the strength of his right arm. Be careful to exert the same amount of pressure each time. Pay attention to the strength of each of the chakras, recording the weak ones. Check all the chakras. First the crown at the top of the head, then the brow at the center of the forehead. Next the throat, then the heart chakra in the center of the chest. Then the solar plexus, just above the stomach. The second or splenic chakra is half-way between the navel and the groin. The root chakra, at the groin, is next. Then, for good measure, the left leg and the right leg. After scanning the body with your crystal and making corrections, muscle test all the chakras once again. You should observe a marked increase in the strength of the body.

Muscle testing is not really a fully scientific method of testing, but it is an excellent way to show an increase in the overall field strength of the body after treatment.

Aura scanning is our preferred method for preparing a client for additional treatment. Since it balances and relaxes the whole body, the client has less resistance to further efforts. It is especially good for chiropractic and massage work where muscle tension and resistance hinder the efforts of the therapist.

This would be a good method for preparing a patient for surgery. Get the energy fields in balance and more energy will be available to overcome the trauma of the operation and to speed the healing process. Do it again after the operation and accelerate the healing even more.

AWARENESS

Awareness implies perception and understanding. The crystal stimulates all the senses, both outer and inner. More information can be brought in by these senses. The crystal increases the capacity of the brain and expands the mind. This promotes a greater understanding of the increased information. The sum of the increases of both data and understanding is an increase in awareness. Awareness is our way of looking at and living in this world. If we enlarge our awareness do we not amplify our personal world? Remember this: as we come to understand the small room of existence we live in, we will find new doors to new rooms of greater size.

MAGIC

The use of ceremony and ritual to affect energy is the major function of magic. Crystals do interact with energy and therefore can and are used in magical ceremonies. Magic is a charged word with many unearned and emotional attachments. If you used the words "Molecular Energy Displacement," would it be more acceptable? Someday we will study the science of magic and find it does have laws, as does all of existence.

PICKING A CRYSTAL

The crystals which are most attuned to you will begin to send out signals to the psychic centers of your brain. The closer you come to the crystal and the longer you are around it, the stronger these connections become. Your logical mind, always seeking a meaning, interprets this as an attraction. You may be drawn because the crystal is large or small, fat or thin, clear, cloudy or colored. Whatever the reason, choose the one to which you are most drawn.

When you want to pick a crystal for someone else, think about them and picture them in your mind. Imagine them picking out a crystal from the selection available. When you see them pick the crystal, open your eyes. Look at the crystals available and pick the one you are attracted to the most. The person for whom you are getting the crystal will choose through the telepathic link between you, formed when you pictured him or her. This is a great technique for choosing any type of gift. People will be amazed at how perceptive you are when you give them what they have always wanted.

WEARING A CRYSTAL

Crystals will amplify the entire energy field of the body. If you wear crystal over a particular area, it will focus more strongly in that area.

If worn close to the neck, crystal will stimulate the thyroid and parathyroid glands. This is excellent for respiratory problems such as congestion and sore throats.

Worn over the heart, crystal stimulates the thymus glands and increases the efficiency of the immune system for defense against disease.

Wearing a crystal over the solar plexus will cause a stimulation in total body energies but also can increase your emotional field. Sometimes this is not wanted.

The most recommended position is over the heart. This can be accomplished by wearing a crystal pendant on a gold or silver chain from 18 to 22 inches long. Much concern has been created over wearing a crystal with the point up or down. We experimented extensively with Kirlian cameras to see if the direction of the point mattered. We found an overall increase in the field energy of the body no matter which way it was pointed — up, down or sideways. None of the directions caused a decrease in the energy field. Pointing the crystal up channeled some of the energy into the upper chakras. This stimulated some and caused others to be out of their bodies, very "spacey." When the crystal was worn horizontally, a small increase was noted in the energy field in front of the body, with a large increase on the sides. When the point was down, there was a slight grounding effect as energy was directed toward the lower body. This had the tendency to bring people back into their bodies. We recommend most people wearing points down to keep better grounded and more in tune with the world. Wear the crystal with the point up when meditating, praying or studying for and taking tests. The rest of the time, wear the point down.

POTPOURRI

GIFTS

Many people have heard they should only use a crystal for healing if it is given to them. The gift of a crystal is a gift of love. It carries the spiritual vibrations of love with it. Healings done with this crystal are more easily achieved through this love vibration. What if you have no one to give you a crystal but you have an intense desire to help others? The desire in your heart will serve to supply the necessary love vibration for spiritual healing. If you are ready and want to use a crystal, by all means buy one. It is not how you get a crystal that matters. It is how you use it.

SHAPES

Tumbling or polishing stones seems to open up and increase the energy in most crystals.

Faceting can determine the way energy flows from a crystal. The angles and shape of the faceting will give direction to the energy.

Crystals formed as pyramids have special properties. They focus and amplify both through the pyramid shape and the molecular structure of the crystal. The pyramid focuses energy in a tight beam through the apex or top. The spiral growth of quartz causes energy to flow out of it in a spiral. When the two are combined, energy will flow from a crystal pyramid in a tight spiral beam which can sometimes be focused more easily.

Crystal balls send energy in all directions. They are the most unified of all shapes.

The egg shape is extremely versatile. Hold the large end up and it can be used for scrying or crystal gazing. Held sideways between the thumb and fingers, it is easy to use for scanning the auric field of the body. Point the small end forward and it can be used for reflexology, zone·therapy and shiatsu or accupressure. The curve of the egg makes it fit perfectly in the curve of the hand for meditation.

Double terminated crystals are multifunctional. Energy can move out in either direction or both directions at once. Herkimer diamonds are double terminated crystals from the Herkimer County area of New York. They are very short, coupled crystals of power and clarity. Double terminated crystals are excellent for astral projection and dreaming. Put them under your pillow at night and they will increase and intensify the dream state.

LEAD CRYSTAL

Lead crystal is created by melting sand and lead and mixing them together. The molecular alignment of this mixture is random and does not have any of the properties of quartz. Hang your lead crystals in the sunlight and enjoy the beautiful rainbows, but wear and use only quartz.

BELIEF

The crystal is solidly founded in physical law. It is not necessary to believe in it for it to work. Since it does function with the mental forces, it is possible for dis-belief to cause a lessening or blocking effect. Belief can smooth the way for the crystals to do their work more efficiently. We subscribe to the statement that belief is getting out of the way of what you want to do.

HOW MANY CRYSTALS?

Everyone should wear one crystal as a pendant resting over the heart. Our tests have shown an increase in the energy field of 200 percent or more when wearing a pendant.

Each person should have a personal meditation crystal. My guidance has recently stated meditation is necessary for **survival** in the new age. Meditation strengthens and harmonizes the auric field, particularly the emotional energy field. Tremendous emotional and physical changes are coming as a part of the movement into the Aquarian Age. Meditation will strengthen our ability to resist or ride with these changes. The crystal intensifies meditation.

Your personal meditation crystal can be used for healing yourself. It should not be used for healing with others. If you work with others in healing, you should have a special crystal for that purpose. If you do advanced therapeutic work you will need two healing crystals.

For showing to others, you may have special sharing crystals — as many as you want or need.

LEFT-HANDEDNESS

Energy moves in the left hand and out the right whether you are left- or right-handed. The techniques described in this book apply to all, exactly as described.

CRYSTALS AND SEX

After survival, the sex drive is the strongest drive we have. It exists and must be dealt with throughout our lives. It is an integral part of our emotional and mental energies. A fully functioning sex life requires a balanced, healthy mind and body. The crystal helps at all levels. Get all the energy centers working in balance and sex will fall into its rightful place as a natural function of being human. If it is weak, it will strengthen. If it is too strong, it will achieve a balance. This is the automatic action of the crystal.

Rose quartz is the stone found most effective for emotional balance for heart problems. Citrine quartz works quite well for balancing the lower energy centers, including the sex center. Wearing either or both stones should help maintain balance.

Future

Before we tread into crystal's future, we want to reiterate that we are in no way connected with the medical profession. We are not doctors — we are researchers, instructors and students ourselves. We are commenting on our findings, we are not advising anyone to stop any type of medical treatment or refrain from going to a doctor. What we are saying is that the mind is a powerful instrument for health and the crystal is a tool that enhances both the mind and good health for those who use it.

For the future we must look into the past. One of the ways to look into the past is to relearn.

What about the future use of crystals? Much research is being carried on all over the world with crystals. Many are recovering the knowledge of crystals from the past — and their use for power generation and anti-gravity. Many are working to re-develop the Wilhelm Reich weather controller, which used crystals. Others continue to refine their designs for space craft and space drives. Everywhere people are experimenting with color, sound, magnets, orgone accumulators and the mind combined with crystals for mental, emotional and physical healing. Several groups are using crystals to open and strengthen their telepathic communication with teachers, masters and healers from other dimensions and worlds by intuitive channeling. One group is working to open communication with plants and animals. Others are speaking to the devas, angels of the mineral, vegetable, animal and human kingdoms.

There is a strong possibility crystals and the human mind can control and eliminate unwanted radiation. We should not leave out the concerted, world-wide effort by major governments, including our own, to develop psychotronic devices for warfare. Remember, you can use fire to cook a meal or burn your house down. Some people want to use crystals to dominate the world as was attempted in Atlantis. This will not be allowed to happen! Together we can use crystals to create a new world of balance, harmony and love. This is the promise of crystals.

For those of you who desire schedules for Crystal Healing Workshops, who have more questions or who simply want to share your experiences, write to DaEl at 110 Second Avenue South, Suite A-13, Pacheco, CA 94553. Please include a business-size, self-addressed, stamped envelope for a workshop schedule.

We have a large selection of cleansed and activated crystals for healing, pain reduction and meditation. We have a lovely selection of gold and silver mounted crystal jewelry for protection and beauty. We will be happy to send you a detailed catalog which includes large clusters, real crystal balls, crystal eggs, pyramids and other energy devices. The Crystal Company, 110 2nd Avenue South, Suite A-13, Pacheco, CA 94553.